Don't Suspend Me!

This book is dedicated to all students at a crossroads in their educational career and/or life, where the path they take will be determined by the decisions educators and administrators make—who either support by teaching behavior or reject by using traditional exclusionary methods. May this book help educators return a student to their correct path where they will have the opportunities to reach their dreams because they were supported behaviorally.

Don't Suspend Me!

An Alternative Discipline Toolkit

Jessica Djabrayan Hannigan

John E. Hannigan

CORWIN
A SAGE Publishing Company

FOR INFORMATION:

Corwin
A SAGE Company
2455 Teller Road
Thousand Oaks, California 91320
(800) 233-9936
www.corwin.com

SAGE Publications Ltd.
1 Oliver's Yard
55 City Road
London EC1Y 1SP
United Kingdom

SAGE Publications India Pvt. Ltd.
B 1/I 1 Mohan Cooperative Industrial Area
Mathura Road, New Delhi 110 044
India

SAGE Publications Asia-Pacific Pte. Ltd.
3 Church Street
#10-04 Samsung Hub
Singapore 049483

Senior Acquisitions Editor: Jessica Allan
Senior Associate Editor: Kimberly Greenberg
Editorial Assistant: Katie Crilley
Production Editor: Melanie Birdsall
Copy Editor: Terri Lee Paulsen
Typesetter: C&M Digitals (P) Ltd.
Proofreader: Laura Webb
Indexer: Amy Murphy
Cover Designer: Candice Harman
Marketing Manager: Jill Margulies

Printed in the United States of America

Library of Congress Cataloging-in-Publication Data

Names: Djabrayan Hannigan, Jessica, author. | Hannigan, John E., author.

Title: Don't suspend me! : an alternative discipline toolkit / Jessica Djabrayan Hannigan, John E. Hannigan.

Description: Thousand Oaks, California : Corwin, a SAGE Company, 2016. | Includes bibliographical references and index.

Identifiers: LCCN 2016011378 | ISBN 9781506350370 (pbk. : alk. paper)

Subjects: LCSH: Rewards and punishments in education. | School discipline. | Problem children—Behavior modification.

Classification: LCC LB3025 .D53 2016 | DDC 371.5—dc23
LC record available at https://lccn.loc.gov/2016011378

This book is printed on acid-free paper.

19 20 21 22 12 11 10 9

Contents

**Part III. Alternative Discipline Menu
by Common Behavior Incidents**

Preface

THE SCHOOL SYSTEM WILL SUPPORT ALL STUDENTS WITH . . .
OUR SCHOOL EXISTS TO PROVIDE ALL STUDENTS A . . .
. . . WHERE THE CHILD COMES FIRST.

You can probably finish the rest of these school or district mission or vision statements, but can you finish them while confidently including the importance of the social-emotional needs of *all* students? To advocate for *all* students when using discipline in an alternative fashion, these commonly used mission or vision statements need to include, " . . . the social-emotional learning of a student is valued as importantly as any academic subject taught in school." Most mission and vision statements say we support *all* students, but do our actions reflect it when it comes to student behavior? Can we support equity for all students and focus on the social-emotional development of a student while using punitive, exclusionary practices as the only means of teaching behavior? Additionally, there is a disproportionality in discipline for students of color when compared to their white counterparts for similar behavior incidents in schools. For there to be equity in school discipline, a belief system is needed that allows educators to advocate for individualized responses to student behavior rather than a one-size-fits-all approach.

We understand the challenge of looking at behavior in the ways described in this book. This book is not based on theory; it is written by practitioners for practitioners and is based on our experiences in changing behavior by using alternatives. The at-risk behavior students on your campus are at a crossroads that will define the direction of their lives. Therefore, the need for innovative methods for addressing discipline is now. Misconceptions arise when the term *alternative discipline* is mentioned; some think of alternative discipline as an excuse to dismiss poor behavior. This is not what is meant by alternative discipline. To help clarify, you need to know what alternative discipline is not.

Alternative discipline is not stopping the suspension of students in order to meet a school or district behavior data quota.

It is using other means of discipline to help students learn from their behaviors rather than sending them home as the first response.

Alternative discipline is not ignoring the stakeholders who have been affected by the student's behavior.

It is working with the stakeholders to help restore what has been damaged and work together to help the student change his or her behavior.

Alternative discipline is not assigning the same discipline for every student without knowing the reason for the misbehavior.

It is taking the time to learn about what triggered the behavior in the first place.

Alternative discipline is not a school that does not have effective behavior systems (foundation) in place to support responding to discipline in this fashion.

It is how discipline is handled in a school that has systems of behavioral supports in place for school-wide, targeted/at-risk groups, and individualized students (special education and general education).

Alternative discipline is not assigned without consistent implementation and follow-through.

It is a method of delivery that requires the administrator and stakeholders to work together and ensure all components of the alternative discipline are put into place and implemented with fidelity.

Alternative discipline is not easy to do.

It is time intensive and requires a belief system in the leader(s) of the school and/or district to create a culture that supports working with students in this fashion.

This book is written to encourage educators to look at discipline from a unique lens. Issues with discipline and challenging behaviors in school tend to provoke negative feelings from educators. We want to help educators take a minute to reflect on what makes discipline frustrating and difficult for stakeholders and feel comfortable with approaching discipline in the way we are suggesting. In order to do so, a school system needs to have a healthy functioning behavioral/social-emotional system designed to respond to the behavioral needs of *all* students. Approaching discipline by only using the traditional approach of suspension is not working for *all* students. Therefore, we challenge educators to be aware of the misconceptions of alternative discipline and really own the words designed to frame a school's or district's identity and culture.

Acknowledgments

We wish to personally thank the following people and organizations for their contributions to our inspiration and knowledge in creating this book: Fresno County Office of Education, Fresno State University, the Sanger Unified School District family, Reagan Elementary teachers and staff, and all schools and districts across the state we have trained to utilize alternative discipline methods. Also, to all of our supervisors, mentors, professors, colleagues, students, friends, and family who have allowed us to innovate and shared in our passion of what we believe in. This would not have been possible without all of you.

To the Djabrayan, Hannigan, Baboyan, and Navo families, we thank you for your endless love, support, and encouragement. A special thank-you to our parents, Bedros and Dzovinar Djabrayan and Mike and Sky Hannigan, for your help and relentless support during this process. And, with love and affection and in memory of our grandmothers, Nene, Grandma Dottie, and Grandma Mar, who helped shape who we have become as adults, educators, and parents.

To our beautiful girls, Riley and Rowan, thank you for all your love and support and always being our number one fans. Through this book, we hope to model for you what it means to set high goals and never give up.

Our appreciation goes to the team at Corwin for recognizing this is a comprehensive and innovative method of addressing and supporting student behaviors. Thank you for giving us the platform to share our voice and help students.

To all who read this book, we thank you for truly doing what is best for *all* students.

About the Authors

Educational consultant **Dr. Jessica Djabrayan Hannigan** works with school districts and county offices in California on designing and implementing effective, successful school and district response to intervention (RTI) behavior systems. She trains schools on the Positive Behavior Interventions and Supports (PBIS) Champion Model System that she designed, focusing on teaching teachers, administrators, and support staff to create behavior RTI systems similar to academic systems in schools. The combination of her student support services/ special education services and school- and district-level administration experiences has allowed her to develop and implement systematic ways for school and district leaders to address the social-emotional needs of students from an innovative perspective. Some of her recognitions include being named Outstanding School Psychologist of the Year, Administrator of the Year, Outstanding Faculty Publications Recipient, and being recognized by the California Legislature Assembly for her work in social justice and equity for the Central Valley. She is an adjunct professor at Fresno State University in the Educational Leadership Department as well as an adjunct faculty member at Fresno Pacific University. She is the coauthor of *The PBIS Tier One Handbook* and an educational consultant for Corwin. Dr. Hannigan resides in Fresno, California, with her husband, John, and stepdaughters, Rowan and Riley.

Dr. John E. Hannigan is currently in his seventh year as principal of Ronald W. Reagan Elementary in Sanger Unified School District, which under his leadership has earned California State Distinguished School, California Title I Academic Achievement Award for closing the achievement gap by the California Department of Education; Gold Ribbon School for model program by the California Department of Education; a 2011, 2012, 2013, and 2014 California Honor Roll school by California Business for Educational Excellence; a 10 out of 10 similar school statewide ranking; 2010, 2012, and 2016 Bonner Award for Character Education; 2013 Silver Level Model School recognition, and 2014, 2015, and 2016 Gold Level Model School recognition from Fresno County Office of Education for Positive Behavioral Interventions and Supports. Dr. Hannigan is Sanger Unified's 2016 Administrator of the Year. He also serves on the Advisory Council for the Dean of California State University, Fresno, Kremen School of Education and Human Development. Dr. Hannigan resides in Fresno, California, with his wife, Jessica, and daughters, Rowan and Riley.

PART 1

The What and Why of Alternative Discipline That Works!

1

Building a Case for Alternative Discipline

"A STUDENT STRUGGLING TO READ IS NOT SENT HOME AND EXPECTED TO RETURN READING FLUENTLY, SO WHY IS IT THAT A STUDENT STRUGGLING TO BEHAVE IS SENT HOME AND EXPECTED TO RETURN BEHAVING DECENTLY?"

The first known use and origin of the word *discipline* dates back to the 13th century from the Latin word *disciplina*, meaning teaching and learning. Today, some define discipline as training that corrects, molds, or perfects the mental faculties or moral character; others define discipline as a verb that means to punish in order to gain control or enforce obedience. While many would disagree on the meaning and purpose of discipline, it remains one of the most commonly stated reasons for not having enough time for effective implementation of school or classroom programs/initiatives. While true, however, using a reactive discipline approach actually takes more time in the long run than a preventive approach. Effective discipline should be designed to improve behavior, rather than dismissing it for a few days through suspension and hoping the student returns to school "fixed." This requires thinking beyond the traditional method of sending students home and hoping that either (a) their parents will teach them not to do it again, or (b) being home from school will teach them not to do it again. In fact, the research demonstrates the contrary. We will begin making our case by comparing the evolution of both academic and behavior systems in schools.

Prior to the Individuals with Disabilities Education Act (IDEA) of 2004, the traditional method of deciding whether a struggling student receives extra time and support through special education was with the *discrepancy model*. Under the discrepancy model, action would not take place until there was a discrepancy between a student's expected achievement and their actual achievement. Simply put, a school had to wait for a student to fail before providing the supports necessary to accelerate learning. Under this model, as McCook (2006, p. 1) states, "It must be the child's fault, or the problem certainly must be the child. Why else would the child have such a discrepancy between expected achievement and actual achievement?" The "wait to fail" model produced a large number of students misidentified as requiring special education services and a disproportionate number of racial minority students misdiagnosed with a learning disability. The introduction of 2004 IDEA allowed schools to use the response to intervention (RTI) framework for identification purposes, which means only after students have failed responding to a series of timely, systematic, increasingly focused, and intensive research-based interventions will a student be considered for special education services. RTI allows schools to identify the kinds of support struggling students need and provide individualized support when it's needed.

Exclusionary discipline practices are equivalent to using the wait-to-fail approach in academics; both are reactionary, not preventive. Having a solid, preventive tier one behavior system in place (see *PBIS Tier One Handbook,* Hannigan & Hauser, 2014) coupled with an innovative response to students who misbehave (this book) does to behavior systems what 2004 IDEA and RTI were designed to do for academic systems.

The traditional mindset about student learning shifted from being the "child's fault" in a discrepancy model toward a belief that all students can and will learn. With this belief, every resource and support is exhausted to provide a student with the resources needed to support learning. However, when it comes to behavior, do we believe that every student can and will behave? Do we exhaust every resource and provide every strategy to support a student in his or her behavior, or do we use suspension as our only means to "teach" a student how to behave? Using suspension is the reactive wait-to-fail model for behavior. Is behavior RTI (preventive discipline) visible on your campus? Or does your system respond to behavior today with the same approach schools responded to academics 15 years ago?

Over the past few decades, methods of disciplining K–12 students have transformed significantly when compared to traditional practices, however, still not to the level it should be.

Specifically, there have been shifts in methods such as corporal punishment, zero tolerance, and use of exclusionary practices such as suspensions and expulsions toward creating positive behavioral environments in schools with the focus on improved student achievement both academically and behaviorally. In analyzing over 20 years of research on discipline approaches, researchers found that out-of-school suspension and zero-tolerance approaches to discipline do not reduce or prevent misbehavior and correlates with lower achievement (Irvin, Tobin, Sprague, Sugai, & Vincent, 2004; Losen, 2011; Mayer, 1995; Skiba & Peterson, 1999; Skiba & Rausch, 2006). In fact, this form of traditional discipline does not make the school feel safer and results in negative outcomes for the child and the community (Skiba & Peterson, 1999). Similarly, Balfanz and Boccanfuso (2007) found that students who were suspended and/or expelled were more likely to be held back a grade or drop out of school. Furthermore, the likelihood of being involved in the juvenile justice system is increased significantly for students addressed with a traditional discipline approach (Leone et al., 2003; Wald & Losen, 2003). Perry and Morris (2014) found that higher levels of exclusionary discipline within schools over time generate collateral damage, negatively affecting the academic achievement of nonsuspended students in punitive contexts. Chard, Smith, and Sugai (1992) summarized discipline practices in education by stating that, "there is one burden that consumes more time, energy, and attention than any other . . . school discipline" (p. 19). Therefore, it is not a surprise that when problem behaviors occur in schools, common practice has been to react in a stringent manner, which has not demonstrated to be successful for all (Chard et al., 1992).

Although there is an abundance of evidence demonstrating the negative effects of suspension, it continues to be the most commonly used method of discipline throughout the nation. We understand choosing alternative forms of discipline will be more challenging and time-consuming in the beginning. Here are some common oppositional messages we hear as we present our approach on discipline. Do any of these messages sound familiar?

But . . .

"I had to make an example out of him."

"I don't have time to do it the other way."

"I want my teachers to know I support them."

"We need to inconvenience the parents."

"I don't want the other parents to feel that nothing was done."

"We need a break from this student."

"Alternatives require more work and are more time-consuming."

"There is no way we have the time or staffing to do this."

"Why not just suspend?"

If you believe it takes too much time to use alternatives and is quicker to send a student home than teach them correct behavior, consider this: A typical major referral takes approximately 45 to 60 minutes of an administrator's time. Suspension does not correct the behavior and will likely repeat, leading to multiple 45- to 60-minute occurrences. Using the incident as a teaching opportunity will reduce the likelihood of a repeated incident, consequently, leading to fewer referrals and significantly decreasing the amount of time spent disciplining.

If preventive and effective discipline is a priority, you will make it a primary initiative at your school. To make this work, it is critical to intentionally create a system designed to support alternative discipline. Here are seven actions to consider to successfully make time for effective discipline:

Belief. As educators, we approach instruction with the belief that every student can and will learn. With this belief, we exhaust every resource and support necessary to improve learning. As an administrator you have to question your own beliefs about discipline. Do you believe every student can and will behave decently? Is every resource and strategy exhausted to support a student in their behavior, or is suspension used as the only means to "teach" a student how to behave? If you believe what you are currently doing is working, there is no compelling reason to change. If you do not believe in preventive discipline, it will not be an expectation nor a priority in your school.

Invest in Preventive Response to Intervention (RTI) Systems for Both Academics and Behavior. Invest in building your school staff's understanding around creating effective systems for responding to students school-wide, targeted/at-risk groups, and individualized both in academics and behavior. Investing here will give you more time to focus on a preventive model rather than reactive. Initial best teaching and best classroom management will support approximately 80% of your students in both academics and behavior. It is also imperative to organize your school's targeted/at-risk and individualized interventions for students who are not responding to the school-wide approach. The PBIS Champion Model is one research-based RTI model that can help you do this at your school.

Visibility and Active Supervision. As an administrator, it is critical to be out of your office and visible to students and staff to build effective relationships and make meaningful connections with students. Active supervision requires an intentional focus on movement, scanning, and positive interactions during supervision; this is essential and needs to be modeled by the administrator. Taking the time to train your staff on visibility and active supervision will save you the time of responding to behavior incidents due to deficiencies in supervision from staff.

Invest in Gaining Faculty Commitment. Take time to educate your staff on alternative discipline approaches. Make it a priority to share school behavior data, gather input from the staff, and work with staff on discipline so they feel part of the process. Share effective discipline success stories with the staff. If you take the time to do this and make yourself available to have difficult ongoing conversations around beliefs, you will see more ownership with staff when handling minor discipline and increased buy-in on major administrator-handled discipline. Communication is also key for staff to understand the logic behind conducting behavior in this structure. In addition, discipline will become a team effort to supporting a student, rather than something only executed and monitored by an administrator.

Create and Nurture a Behavior Team. It is critical for every school to have a behavior team designed to set behavior goals, establish and monitor behavior interventions, and to support preventive systems work. An administrator who provides a team the opportunity to meet on a regular basis to discuss school-wide, targeted/small group, and individualized behavior data and trends will benefit. This allows for data to be used to provide interventions for students by name, by need, instead of after they've escalated to the next level of discipline. Make sure the social-emotional experts on campus, such as a school counselor or school psychologist, are an active part of the behavior team. Designate this time with your behavior team; use a monitoring tool to ensure data is used to identify and monitor the progress of focus students. The emphasis here is to get to the students before they get to you.

Create a Toolkit of Effective Discipline. Organize preventive discipline ideas in a toolkit for future reference. As you conduct discipline in this manner, you will begin using a set of actions you tend to assign; therefore, if you have another similar incident, you can reference your toolkit to help save time. The alternatives in this book are designed to give options and examples of alternative forms of discipline used to correct misbehavior. As you see how students respond to alternatives, you will think of other innovative alternatives to use. In the event of another similar-type incident at the school, the administrator can reference their toolkit for consequences/interventions instead of creating another.

Supporting a System for Alternatives. Make sure the alternative discipline you assign is implemented with fidelity and effectively communicated to all stakeholders. Understand that establishing this will require time and human capital to implement and monitor with success. Although it may be challenging to allocate so many resources for one student, the ultimate goal is to help the student learn and change his/her behavior. Without an intentional focus on alternatives, the student will continue taking away time from your staff throughout the school year with continuing behavior challenges, since the function of the student's behavior was never addressed. Teaching desired outcomes through alternatives to suspension will reduce the frequency of repeat offenses, thus creating less time dealing with discipline than using suspension alone.

2

Discipline Belief Self-Inventory

The Discipline Belief Self-Inventory will provide educators with a look into their individual beliefs about discipline. Inventory statements are derived from an analysis of administrator responses across all grade levels and a range of differences between traditional and innovative/alternative discipline beliefs and/or approaches.

WHO IS THIS SELF-INVENTORY FOR?

Educators—such as teachers, school support staff, and school- and district-level administrators—who want to create effective behavior systems in their schools can benefit from this self-inventory. This inventory can also aid future educators and leaders to reflect on their discipline beliefs.

WHY DOES THIS SELF-INVENTORY MATTER TO ME?

We have found through our research and work with practitioners the primary reason alternative discipline does not work is the beliefs of the administrator at the school or district, the person responsible for establishing the school's culture. If the leader does not believe in alternative discipline methods, they (1) will implement the discipline ineffectively, resulting in a lack of buy-in from the staff and stakeholders, and (2) cannot justify the importance for students to be given the chance to learn behaviors similar to how they learn academics. Your school or district will not succeed in supporting behavior unless your beliefs about discipline shift to support it.

WHAT ARE YOUR CURRENT BELIEFS ABOUT DISCIPLINE?

Please review the statements and rate yourself on your discipline beliefs. Please be honest in your responses. Remember, this self-inventory is anonymous and designed to serve as a reflection and self-awareness of where you currently fall in your beliefs about discipline.

Discipline Belief Self-Inventory

1. Suspensions work to change student behavior.

1	2	3	4	5
Strongly Disagree				Strongly Agree

2. Discipline should be used as a teaching opportunity.

1	2	3	4	5
Strongly Disagree				Strongly Agree

3. I prefer a black-and-white discipline handbook with exact number of days outlined for suspensions based on behavior.

1	2	3	4	5
Strongly Disagree				Strongly Agree

4. Behavior should be addressed in an individualized fashion.

1	2	3	4	5
Strongly Disagree				Strongly Agree

5. Parents need to be inconvenienced with suspensions.

1	2	3	4	5
Strongly Disagree				Strongly Agree

6. Restorative, reflective, and instructional opportunities should be part of the consequence/intervention.

1	2	3	4	5
Strongly Disagree				Strongly Agree

7. Students should be suspended when teachers or stakeholders pressure me to suspend.

1	2	3	4	5
Strongly Disagree				Strongly Agree

8. I monitor student behavior on an ongoing basis.

1	2	3	4	5
Strongly Disagree				Strongly Agree

9. I use suspension to set an example.

1	2	3	4	5
Strongly Disagree				Strongly Agree

10. I find the function of the behavior and innovate a consequence based on identified function.

1	2	3	4	5
Strongly Disagree				Strongly Agree

(Continued)

(Continued)

11. I need to be convinced to use alternative discipline approaches.

1	2	3	4	5
Strongly Disagree				Strongly Agree

12. I involve parents, teachers, and other stakeholders with the assigned discipline.

1	2	3	4	5
Strongly Disagree				Strongly Agree

13. There is not enough time to do alternative discipline.

1	2	3	4	5
Strongly Disagree				Strongly Agree

14. I establish a relationship with the student throughout the alternative discipline process.

1	2	3	4	5
Strongly Disagree				Strongly Agree

15. I avoid difficult conversations about alternative discipline decisions.

1	2	3	4	5
Strongly Disagree				Strongly Agree

16. I provide a consequence/intervention in lieu of suspension.

1	2	3	4	5
Strongly Disagree				Strongly Agree

17. I prefer to send students home instead of keeping them at school.

1	2	3	4	5
Strongly Disagree				Strongly Agree

18. I am confident enough to justify the reasoning behind using alternative discipline.

1	2	3	4	5
Strongly Disagree				Strongly Agree

19. I demonstrate support to teachers by suspending students.

1	2	3	4	5
Strongly Disagree				Strongly Agree

20. I am comfortable with my skills to build believers in alternative discipline by demonstrating positive effects of using alternatives.

1	2	3	4	5
Strongly Disagree				Strongly Agree

DISCIPLINE BELIEF 💼
SELF-INVENTORY SCORING

Scoring Note: If the combination of your odd and even point ranges do not fall into a disciplinarian category, please consider the following: (a) retake the inventory to make sure you are not contradicting yourself in your ratings, or (b) consider yourself in the emergent range due to the similarity of your scores supporting both traditional and innovative discipline beliefs.

Total odd questions: _____   **Total even questions:** _____

Traditional Disciplinarian: A traditional disciplinarian is a disciplinarian who prefers the black-and-white discipline handbook as a guide to how to conduct discipline. This type of disciplinarian believes this form of discipline works and prefers taking the safe route with a business-as-usual approach to discipline.

*Total odd questions in the 40- to 50-point range **and***
Total even questions in the 10- to 20-point range

Emergent Disciplinarian: An emergent disciplinarian is inconsistent with his/her discipline practices. This type of disciplinarian assigns discipline based on his/her disposition and/or pressures from others. This type of disciplinarian does not have a strong belief about discipline one way or another. An emergent disciplinarian will experiment with alternative discipline methods but does not have the skill set or tools to do so. This usually results in using alternatives ineffectively.

*Total odd questions in the 21- to 39-point range **and***
Total even questions in the 21- to 39-point range

Innovative Disciplinarian: An innovative disciplinarian believes in teaching behavior similar to teaching academics. This type of disciplinarian will innovate based on discipline incidents and takes the time to assign, implement, and monitor effective discipline. This type of disciplinarian is confident in having difficult conversations about behavior and has the ability to work with stakeholders on appropriate assignment of discipline that addresses the behavior.

*Total odd questions in the 10- to 20-point range **and***
Total even questions in the 40- to 50-point range

3

Questions and Tips Before You Begin

EVERYTHING USED IN THIS TOOLKIT IS BASED ON NEEDS FROM EDUCATORS WE WORK WITH. THIS BOOK IS WRITTEN BY PRACTITIONERS FOR PRACTITIONERS. THESE AREN'T THEORIES OR SUGGESTIONS BASED ON WHAT WE THINK MAY WORK. HERE ARE THE MOST COMMONLY ASKED QUESTIONS.

IS ALTERNATIVE DISCIPLINE A ONE-SIZE-FITS-ALL APPROACH?

No, this book is designed to give educators a guideline to address discipline based on individual student behavioral needs. Educators assigning discipline need to establish relationships with their students to understand their needs and what they respond to prior to approaching discipline in this fashion. The examples provided are based on common discipline incidents with alternative methods and demonstrated to be effective in changing behavior. The suggested alternatives for each incident are designed to be thought provoking and can be expanded based on grade-level appropriateness and aligned with available resources at your school. We have found sharing ideas helps generate ideas for what works across schools and can also be adjusted to meet the needs of individual cases. We understand each student is different, which is why we argue against a traditional black-and-white suspension handbook because it takes away the ability to use individualized consequences for students. This toolkit is designed to help educators assign discipline "by name, by need" for each student and incident versus the traditional three- to five-day suspension response to an incident.

ARE CONVERSATIONS ABOUT USING ALTERNATIVE DISCIPLINE DIFFICULT TO HAVE?

Yes, communicating alternative discipline effectively can be a laborious task for administrators. Prior to giving an alternative to a student, the beliefs of the administrator must support it. If the administrator cannot articulate the significance of why the alternative is important, nobody on that campus will believe it to be important. There is an art to assigning appropriate discipline while working with the stakeholders (parents, teachers, students) and deciding consequences that are appropriate for a student that will change behavior. We want to be clear: The message simply isn't to *not* suspend. The message is this student is returning to your school regardless, so what are you doing to teach and ensure these behaviors are not repeating on your campus? Students would prefer to go home for a few days than deal with alternative consequences. When approaching discipline in this way, one of the most common questions you will hear is, "why didn't you just suspend this student?" Here are some strategies that will help guide difficult conversations around alternative forms of discipline:

Listen to the Stakeholders. Allow the stakeholders to vent and hear them out so you can rationalize what they are saying. They've just experienced the behavior that led to the referral and aren't in a place to listen to an alternative. Allow them to cool down so you can talk them through. Provide them with a safe opportunity to honestly share what they feel. If you do not do this, they will not buy in and the conversation will continue in the staff lounge without you.

Communicate in a Timely Manner. When a teacher sends a student to the office on a referral, they are expecting the behavior to be addressed and a consequence handed out. If the teacher sees the student return to class shortly thereafter, their impression of the outcome will be that the administrator simply said, "don't do that again, now go back to class." A teacher who is not communicated with will feel the incident was dismissed and not handled. It is essential to make it an expectation for yourself to communicate the consequence in a timely manner (same day).

Involve the Teacher in the Alternative and Use It to Teach. When time permits, involve the teacher in creating consequences. It will empower the teacher as an authoritarian in the eyes of the student and someone who levies consequences. It will also bolster the teacher's beliefs around using discipline as a means to teach behavior. Additionally, it will allow them to see how much time and effort goes into doing discipline in this fashion. If they are given the opportunity to be included in the process, it will increase buy-in and support from the teacher.

Liken Behavior to Academics—Behavior RTI/Academic RTI. It is important to articulate the relationship between how adults respond to students who struggle to learn with how they respond to students who struggle to behave. When stakeholders hear the rationale behind why teaching academics is similar to teaching behavior, they are more willing to shift their thinking about how the discipline should be handled. A student struggling to read is not sent home for a few days and expected to return reading; likewise, a student struggling to behave needs more support to change behavior rather than suspension.

Question Beliefs. Be prepared for tough conversations about discipline and beliefs. It is important to get to the core beliefs of the teacher in order to help them work through and support an effective alternative consequence. One helpful method to peel the layers and get to the root/function of the problem behavior and possible solutions is sequential questioning. For example:

Why do you want this student suspended out of your class? He is being defiant.

Why is he being defiant? Because I told him to stop talking and complete his assignment and he didn't.

How did calmly giving him directions trigger the defiance? I yelled it out in front of the class because I was frustrated.

Why have you not asked for help with this student? I didn't want it to seem like I don't know how to handle my class.

Why do you think suspending him from your class today is going to change his behavior when he comes back tomorrow? I don't. I needed to make a point and show him who's boss.

Do you think you made your point? No, actually, I don't. I just needed a break.

Let's work together on a long-term consequence/intervention so you do not have to continue feeling this way.

If we are not forced to question our beliefs about discipline, we cannot get to the level of accepting alternative discipline in place of traditional methods.

💼 HOW CAN WE APPROACH DISCIPLINE IN THIS WAY IF WE DO NOT HAVE THE BUDGET, RESOURCES, AND PERSONNEL FOR IT?

We realize not all schools have the same level of support staff. We've seen schools make this work without a school psychologist or counselor; a two- or five-day-a-week school psychologist and/or counselor; an assistant principal; or none of the above and only a site principal. Ultimately, a school's response to discipline rests with those who make the decision whether a student goes home on a suspension or stays on campus. If suspension is your answer, is the student coming back to your campus when the suspension ends? If so, what are you doing to prevent the behavior from repeating? We would argue simply using a reactive approach to discipline takes more time and human capital from a site than a preventive approach. Furthermore, state and federal regulations include supports for social-emotional learning that align with this framework for discipline. If a school wants to make preventive discipline work, a goal can be written into their school site plan and schools may use funding to support this initiative to decrease suspension and improve the culture at their school. However, this is a common excuse for administrators who do not yet believe in this method. If they invest in creating a school-wide behavior system with the Champion Model (RTI behavior), they will see a decrease in the number of major incidents that occur at their school that require using alternative methods.

DO THE PROVIDED ALTERNATIVE DISCIPLINE EXAMPLES PERTAIN TO ALL GRADE LEVELS?

Yes, the examples provided are based on real-life alternative discipline examples from elementary, secondary, and alternative education settings. As the educator, you can take the suggested alternatives and differentiate them to make them fit for your particular grade level. For example, two students getting into a fight during a soccer game in elementary school is different than two high school students getting into a fight during football practice; however, the suggested alternatives to helping restore and reteach appropriate behaviors will work for both.

IS IT HARDER TO APPROACH DISCIPLINE IN THIS WAY?

Yes, using alternatives is a more difficult way of responding to discipline. It requires individualized attention to the student(s) that is fundamentally different than being sent home for a few days and expecting them to return behaving. Alternatives use discipline to teach behavior similar to how we teach academics. Using alternatives can be challenging. Expect to be challenged by stakeholders (parents, teachers, and district leadership). Communication is essential; obviously due to student confidentiality, you cannot communicate a student's consequences to any parent other than their own. However, it is necessary to let the teacher know what you plan to use as an alternative to get buy-in and involve them in the process. We would recommend including your district's supervisor of Child Welfare and Attendance or area administrator from the district when using alternatives for more serious infractions. Some districts still have zero-tolerance board policies and outdated handbooks that are years behind a belief system built around supporting students when it comes to behavior. As an administrator in this setting, you will want to explain the incident and how you intend to handle it with your direct supervisor to gain support until policies catch up to using alternatives.

🧰 WHEN DO WE USE ALTERNATIVE DISCIPLINE?

Use alternative discipline any time you want to teach and change behavior and incidents where a student would return to your school from a suspension. We understand there are times when students will be placed into an alternative setting or other more serious consequences for their behavior. However, even when a student is placed in an alternative setting and will not return to your campus, we suggest that the alternative discipline still take place in their new setting. Moving the problem behavior does not resolve the fact that the student still needs the opportunity in their new alternative setting to learn how to behave appropriately.

4

Alternative/ Innovative Discipline

As school administrators, we have both experienced the emotions and challenges connected with students making poor decisions in schools that result in school discipline/consequences. We have also experienced the pushback from teachers, parents, and district leadership that comes with not following a black-and-white handbook approach to discipline (*Cautionary note: We are not saying a district should not have general disciplinary guidelines to follow; we are saying the handbook should be updated to include a comprehensive response to student behavior, rather than a one-size-fits-all approach*). This requires thinking beyond the traditional method of sending students home and hoping that their parents will teach them not to do it again or being home from school will teach them not to do it again. It also requires that the message to students, teachers, and parents isn't "we just don't suspend anymore." Opponents to alternatives argue the message sent to students who misbehave is that there are no consequences for their actions because they know they won't be suspended. We would argue, if that is the culture of your school, you aren't using alternatives effectively. When used correctly, the alternative will be much more impactful and meaningful than simply sending a student home for a few days. When a school is firmly grounded in a solid tier one school-wide system for behavior (see *PBIS Tier One Handbook,* Hannigan & Hauser, 2014) and utilizes effective alternatives that are restorative, reflective, and instructional, you will see a dramatic reduction in the number of incidents and a significant increase in the positive culture on your campus. Innovative discipline teaches students real-life lessons and the impact their behavior has on others, the community, and their future. We have an obligation to help students become productive members of the community by preparing them academically as well as social-emotionally to succeed.

💼 WHAT IS ALTERNATIVE/ INNOVATIVE DISCIPLINE?

Alternative/innovative discipline is a framework for assigning meaningful discipline to students. Alternative/innovative discipline has to include a restorative, reflective, and instructional component. Administrators can use any combination of the three (two restorative, two instructional, and one reflective); there isn't a secret formula for how many of each to use as long as you include all three. This framework is centered around two questions: (1) Is this a discipline incident that is resulting in the student returning back to my campus? If yes, an innovative disciplinarian will use an alternative form of discipline, rather than simply sending the student home on a suspension; and (2) Does the consequence have real-life application and meaning to help improve student behavior? The consequence needs to be meaningful for the student. The only way it will be meaningful is if the administrator or educator listens to the student to learn the function of the behavior and establishes a relationship with the student throughout the alternative discipline process.

For the purpose of this book we define restorative, reflective, and instructional as follows:

Restorative: Provide opportunities for the student to restore relationships between themselves and stakeholder(s) they have affected due to the behavior incident (apology, student contracts, community service, restitution, etc.).

Reflective: Provide opportunities for students to reflect about the decisions they made that led to the discipline (reflection sheets, role-playing, interviews, etc.).

Instructional: Provide teaching opportunities for students that target the function of the behavior and helps them learn the skills needed to not engage in such behaviors again (behavior lessons, social skills, teaching opportunities, behavior exams, etc.).

Discipline must be viewed as an opportunity to teach and change behavior. Consequences must be strategically planned and intentionally implemented based on each student by name, by need the same way a school system responds to a student who struggles to learn academically. As you can imagine, this approach is much more time-consuming for an administrator; however, seeing a student's behavior change because you believed in them is equally as fulfilling as seeing a student learn because a teacher believed in and supported them. In Part II, you will find case study examples of how to assign alternative discipline. Part III provides a menu of alternative discipline options for the most common behavior incidents in schools that result in suspensions. Part IV will help you organize what you have learned and bring it all together.

PART II

Case Studies on Alternative Discipline

5

Case Studies

In this chapter, you will find three case study examples of alternative discipline in action. This will allow you to see how the menu of alternative discipline suggestions can be translated through these specific case study examples. It is important to understand that conducting alternative discipline requires more time and resources, therefore, it is critical to first create an effective tiered behavior system at your school so fewer students will engage in behaviors that result in this type of discipline. Taking the time to invest in this type of discipline will decrease the chances of the behaviors reoccurring.

You will also notice the alternative discipline in the highlighted case studies include at least one restorative, one reflective, and one instructional example in the assigned discipline and organized into phases. As you read these case studies, visualize your school setting and resources available to you to address discipline in this way.

Ask yourself the following reflective questions as you read each case study:

1. Does the assigned alternative discipline seem effective?

2. Would you consider assigning discipline in this way?

3. What steps do you need to take to create a culture at your school to discipline in this way?

4. Do you think this type of discipline is more valuable than sending students home?

5. What will be your first step in implementing discipline in this way?

ALTERNATIVE DISCIPLINE CASE STUDY 1

During recess, two sixth-grade male students began arguing over the rules during a football game. This topic has been an ongoing debate between these two boys for the past several weeks. On this particular day, the students were yelling at each other during the game, which attracted a crowd. The yard duty teacher noticed the commotion and was able to intervene. She pulled the boys aside and had them apologize to each other and made them agree not to engage in such behavior again. Both boys agreed to follow the rules, but they were not over the conflict from the game. Although the yard duty teacher believed she had resolved the conflict, she did not realize that one of the students did not know how to get over what he believed to be an injustice and had his friends tell the other boy to meet him in the bathroom after school to fight. The other boy did not want to meet him, but was taunted by his peers to do so throughout the school day. After school, he reluctantly met in the bathroom and engaged in a fight to resolve the issue from the morning football game. The administrator got word of the fight and was able to intervene shortly after it started. After stopping the fight, the administrator had a choice to make about the consequence given. She knew both of these boys and had dealt with them through suspensions in the past, so she challenged herself to try something different knowing her other methods were not effective up to this point. She wanted to make sure the consequence was one that would teach the importance of handling conflict appropriately in the future. Traditionally, she would have referenced the school discipline handbook and suspended them both for three days but decided to look at this discipline differently.

Innovative/Alternative Discipline

Below is the response from the administrator that changed behavior for both students as well as how she approached discipline from this point on. The handling of this incident was also a catalyst to how students and staff at her school viewed the commitment to changing behavior. In the past, she would have used the short conflict resolution script she was trained to use for incidents similar to this one, but she decided to take it several steps deeper into the conflict and resolution. Her steps were simple and to the point with the students. She brought the boys into her office and explained the phases of their consequence. After hearing them, one student actually said he would prefer to be suspended than have to complete all the alternative components of the consequence. He told the administrator he had been suspended plenty of times before and at least this way the consequence would be over when he came back to school. The administrator asked the student if being suspended helped change his behavior. The boy answered, "for a little bit, until someone else made me mad." So she decided at this point to use innovative/alternative discipline that was designed to help change behavior for the long term.

Phase 1 (Restorative): Together, they began by completing a restorative behavior contract with each other. Each student had to share where they felt an injustice took place, write an apology to each other, commit to a resolution, and agree to the progress monitoring terms of the agreement they created together. Both students along with the administrator signed the document.

Phase 2 (Instructional): They were assigned six sessions each of hands-off academy. Hands-off academy was designed to provide a behavior teaching opportunity for both students to learn other methods of resolving conflict rather than through violence. In these courses, the administrator taught coping strategies to the students when dealing with conflict and checked the application of learned skills through behavior scenarios and a culminating behavior exam.

Phase 3 (Reflective): The students had a set check-in date and time with the administrator on a weekly basis where they had to progress monitor their restorative contract and learn about each other. They were asked to both derive 30 questions they wanted answered about each other, interview each other, and prepare a presentation about the other student. This allowed them to have a safe space to learn about the other and how to accept similarities and differences.

Phase 4 (Instructional): Both boys were assigned a project aligned with sports game rules and character. They had to present the rules of the football game to the sixth-grade class and provide strategies for students to use when they become upset during a sports game. In addition, they had to become referees of the football game and focus on identifying students playing the game by the rules and showing character.

Phase 5 (Restorative): Both boys were celebrated for their hard work learning from this major behavior incident at their school. They both had to write a reflection about what they learned from this experience and create an individual contract ensuring they would not engage in this type of behavior again.

ALTERNATIVE DISCIPLINE CASE STUDY 2

A female middle school student noticed the vice principal dropped her cell phone during supervision. Instead of picking it up and giving it back to the administrator, she decided to keep it for herself. In her next two class periods, she bragged about stealing the cell phone while going through the pictures and text messages. An anonymous student reported what she heard in class to the administrator. The administrator was able to conduct an investigation that led to her retrieving her cell phone from the student. However, when she called the mother of the student to report what happened and explained she would be assigning traditional discipline (suspension), the mother told the administrator her daughter had not stolen the phone but in fact she had just purchased it for her. The administrator confirmed with the mother that this was her phone and it was stolen. This parent's defense of her child's theft confirmed that sending the student home on a suspension would not teach correct behavior, so the administrator provided an alternative, real-world consequence for theft.

Phase 1 (Restorative): The administrator met with the student and discussed why she stole the cell phone in the first place. The administrator walked the student through a restorative agreement contract, so it was clear how taking another person's property impacts others. Together, they developed an agreement and began their plan on moving forward to restore the injustice that had taken place.

Phase 2 (Instructional): The student had to research the consequences of stealing in the community. She was assigned a five-paragraph essay that had to include evidence from at least four sources. The topic prompt she had to respond to was as follows: What are ways to earn trust back from a person(s) you have stolen from? What are consequences of this type of behavior in the community? What have you learned from this experience? The essay needed to be signed off by the administration and address all provided prompts.

Phase 3 (Reflective): The student was assigned an apology letter to complete for the administrator and teacher of the classroom she had interrupted by bragging about the incident.

Phase 4 (Restorative): The student was assigned a mentor on campus to provide support through weekly check-ins to ensure the student is on track. The student has input on who the mentor will be (an adult she respects). The student is assigned community service with a time span aligned with cost of stolen item and will be signed off by the community service mentor and administrator upon completion of hours.

Phase 5 (Reflective): The student will create and sign a contract ensuring this behavior will never take place again in the school or community.

💼 ALTERNATIVE DISCIPLINE CASE STUDY 3

A high school male student showed inappropriate pictures of females to other students in class on his cell phone. He also made inappropriate sexual comments to female students in class and throughout campus. He specifically enjoyed making sexual comments to a female student he had a crush on and was not understanding that she did not like the attention he was giving her. It made her feel unsafe at school and anxious to be in class with him.

Phase 1 (Restorative): The administrator conducted a restorative agreement with the two students in a safe space. During this session, the female student was able to tell him how his actions made her feel, with the administrator facilitating. Together, they agreed on a contract to be monitored by the administrator on an ongoing basis.

Phase 2 (Restorative): The male student was assigned to write apology letters to the female student, the teacher, and the parents of the female student. In addition, if consent is received, he will make a personal phone call to the parents of the female student or personally meet with them (with the administrator present) to make certain their daughter feels safe at school and these behaviors will end.

Phase 3 (Reflective): The student will interview three important women in his life about how they would feel if someone showed them inappropriate pictures of women and constantly made sexual comments to them. He had to present his findings from the interviews to the administrator.

Phase 4 (Instructional): The student will read the district handbook description on sexual harassment and identify a sexual harassment description in a work environment within the community. Specifically, he will have to research sexual harassment laws within the field of work he plans to be employed in the future. He will have to write an essay describing what he has learned from these descriptions. The essay will report what he has learned through this research and what the consequences would be for his career and within the community if he continued to engage in these types of behaviors as an adult.

Phase 5 (Instructional): He had to participate in four sessions with a school counselor to role-play appropriate ways to respectfully seek peer attention from female students. In these sessions, he was provided scenarios and taught strategies to handle them appropriately.

Phase 6 (Restorative): He had to meet with the female student in a safe place with the administrator present and share what he learned from this experience. He will also create an individual behavior contract identifying his commitment to changing his behavior.

AUTHORS' NOTE 💼

Consistency and follow-through are critical when assigning alternatives. If any of the above alternatives highlighted through these case studies had an administrator tell a student he or she had to complete an assigned consequence but did not hold the student accountable to completing it, the results are as bad as doing nothing at all. The student will now not fear repeating their behavior because they know their administrator will not back up words with action. This is actually more counterproductive than suspension because now the student does not view the administrator as credible or consistent and all talk with no action. The administrator will also lose the credibility of the staff who were told the alternatives assigned, but see that only parts of it were followed.

PART III

Alternative Discipline Menu by Common Behavior Incidents

6

Alternative Discipline Menu Introduction

This chapter will provide examples of alternative discipline from common discipline incidents in all school settings. It is designed to help you generate ideas for alternative discipline that will work at your school site. **Is the student returning to your school?** We understand some serious behavior incidents will result in a student's removal from a campus. The examples in this chapter are common suspendable incidents in which a student returns to school after serving a suspension. If the student is being placed in an alternative setting (i.e., Community Day School, Continuation School, Alternative Education, or Opportunity Program), the student should still receive the alternative discipline in their new setting as part of their transition, if possible.

This chapter is designed to bridge the gap between a traditional administrator to an innovative administrator when it comes to discipline. Student behavior will change when using these strategies as opposed to simply relying on suspension. When you see student behavior change, your beliefs around discipline will change along with it, then you will begin thinking of your own innovative/alternative methods that will transform the culture of your school.

Alternative discipline resources will be provided after each behavior incident menu of suggestions. Resources used as examples in one menu aren't the only places they can be used and can be cross-referenced across other menu examples when appropriate or adjusted to meet appropriate grade-level needs. As you use this chapter to frame alternative discipline for incidents at your school, remember to include at least one restorative, one reflective, and one instructional example. Accountability for implementation of the assigned alternatives are key to its success. **Discipline assignments and supports need to be consistently in place and monitored to completion to get the positive outcomes you wish to see.** A lack of follow-through from the administrator assigning discipline will diminish student, staff, and stakeholder buy-in and create unintended negative outcomes. Our research has shown that a lack of administrator beliefs and inconsistency of implementation will lead to ineffective results. Administrators in such environments will say, "We tried using alternatives and they don't work." Consistent implementation from effective administrators has been proven to show tremendous success in changing student behavior. It's not that the alternatives don't work; it's that ineffective implementation, weak systems, or beliefs aren't in place to support it.

It is also important to archive what you have attempted to change in a student's behavior. It will also be helpful in demonstrating that the school has exhausted its resources to support a student behaviorally. If it comes to a Student Success Team or Individualized Education Plan meeting to problem solve next steps with the student, this will be important data to support decisions to move a student from perhaps a tier two to tier three behavior intervention. Documentation is also important to give a student continued support from grade to grade or school to school. As a student matriculates from an elementary setting to middle school to high school, it is critical for each new setting to have access to what the student has or has not responded to.

Create an alternative behavior toolkit (either a binder or electronic format) to reference for alternative discipline assignments. This will help you expand on the resources used in this book. As you transition to an innovative discipline administrator, you will learn what we refer to as the art of discipline, which will result in thinking differently when approaching behavior incidents at your school. Rather than being on discipline autopilot and assigning suspensions, you will think of alternative scenarios for incidents, create opportunities for students to learn from their behaviors, and connect the discipline to real-life consequences that change behaviors for the long term. Collaborate with your school psychologist, school counselor, behavior intervention specialist, district office behavior experts, general education and special education teachers, community resources, and any other school or district employees who have expertise in behavior to assist in establishing an effective behavior toolkit. In the next chapter, you will find the alternative discipline menu for common behavior incidents in schools.

Alternative
Discipline Menu

Behavior Incident

BULLYING

Suggestions for Alternatives

Restorative: Student will complete a restorative contract with the other student, getting to the root of the problem and monitored by administration with six to eight weekly check-in points to determine if the contract agreed upon is being followed.

Restorative: Student will be assigned 10 days of restitution for the student who was bullying (restitution to be completed during social time, before school, breaks, lunch, after school). An adult "boss" or supervisor will be assigned who will help supervise the restitution and assignment(s).

Instructional: Student will research bullying and tolerance and create a slide presentation (e.g., PowerPoint, Prezi, Google Slides) to teach other peers about bully prevention (e.g., lessons on relationships, how behaviors impact others, what behaviors will help them with making friends, learning empathy).

Restorative: Apology letters will be written to all stakeholders impacted— other student, administration, parent(s) of the other student.

Reflective: Student bullying will be actively supervised to ensure he or she is following the contract (full school privileges back only after all consequences and assignments are completed).

Instructional: Student will be assigned six sessions of bullying prevention lessons, scenarios, and application opportunities.

Reflective: Student will complete a behavior exam to demonstrate understanding and application of learned skills.

Restorative: Students will revisit the restorative contract at least four times once a week with administrator or designee suppervision.

Instructional: Communication and monitoring with parents of the students to work together to ensure the bullying is no longer taking place (providing parents with strategies to monitor and help at home).

Reflective: After 10 good days following the contract and schedule, the student bullying will get a few privileges back; in 10 more days, the student will receive complete privileges back, but be required to check in on a bi-weekly basis with administration to ensure the bullying has stopped.

Restorative: Students will be assigned a joint project (e.g., creating an antibullying video for the school) with the supervision of the administrator or designee.

For the student being bullied (additional suggestions to consider):

- Establish a safe zone on campus for him or her to go to
- Check in with student throughout the day
- Supervision of the contract and expectations
- Possible counseling (e.g., strategies for her or him to cope)
- Possibly working with the student who bullied him or her on a common project (you would have to monitor and give them a safe zone to work together)

Apology Letter Template

Write an apology letter that includes the following components:

- ❏ Address the stakeholder(s) you have impacted due to your behavior
- ❏ Identify and own the behavior that put you in this position
- ❏ Acknowledge the hurt you may have caused due to your behavior
- ❏ Identify the function of your behavior
- ❏ Express your apology to the stakeholder(s)
- ❏ Provide three examples of what you have learned from this experience
- ❏ Provide three examples demonstrating what will prevent you from engaging in this type of behavior again
- ❏ Assure the stakeholder(s) this will never happen again
- ❏ Sign the letter as a contract to your apology
- ❏ Write five things you like and respect about the person you bullied; provide evidence to support each of the five

Project Assignment Template

Problem Behavior: Bullying

Possible Function of Behavior: Jealousy, lack of social skills

Date to Complete By: _____

Project Assignment

1. Research two local or national newspaper articles that highlight bullying and respond to the following writing prompts: What were commonalities between the articles? What are some ways to prevent bullying? What have you learned from this assignment?

   _____

   _____

   _____

   _____

2. Research laws on bullying. List three laws created to prevent bullying. Provide examples of how to follow the laws.

   _____

   _____

   _____

   _____

3. Develop a project to create bullying prevention awareness. Project needs to include the definition of bullying, ways to prevent bullying, and lessons learned.

   _____

   _____

   _____

   _____

Administrator Signature: _____

Stakeholder Signature(s): _____

Student(s) Signature: _____

Restorative Contract Monitoring Form

Date of Check-In	How are we doing? ☺ ☹	Students' Signatures	Administrator or Designee Signatures
	Circle one: ☺ ☹		
	Circle one: ☺ ☹		
	Circle one: ☺ ☹		
	Circle one: ☺ ☹		
	Circle one: ☺ ☹		
	Circle one: ☺ ☹		
	Circle one: ☺ ☹		

Incentive when goal is met: If we can complete six to eight weeks of positive check-in ratings we will get to have a special lunch with the administrator and each student can invite a friend.

Behavior Incident

 # CYBERBULLYING

Suggestions for Alternatives

Instructional: Student will research federal laws related to cyberbullying, provide a summary of at least three identified laws, and present findings to the administrator.

Reflective: Student will write an article to submit to the school news or local news on how to help students stop cyberbullying.

Instructional: Student will complete six sessions with a designated employee to learn social skills to express feelings without using cyberbullying, which will include role-play practice opportunities.

Restorative: Student will complete a restorative contract between the students and daily check-ins with the administrator for six weeks.

Reflective: Student will create a pamphlet to help create awareness of cyberbullying based on research from cyberbullying case studies.

Restorative: Student will write apology letters to all stakeholders.

Reflective: The student will facilitate a student social media contract with the class or other students.

Instructional: Student will research the impacts of cyberbullying on students and their families and write a two-page paper explaining what was found and how to prevent this from happening.

Restorative: The student will assist the librarian, teacher, or computer technology assistant with keeping the school computers clean from any inappropriate content (10 days).

Instructional: The student will complete a book study/report on cyberbullying.

Social Media Exercise and Pledge

What is the purpose of social media (Facebook, Twitter, Instagram, etc.)?

_____

_____

What is cyberbullying?

_____

_____

Is bullying on social media against the law?

_____

_____

Do your messages or pictures disappear when you delete them?

_____

_____

What are five things you are committing to that will make sure cyberbullying does not happen?

1. _____

2. _____

3. _____

4. _____

5. _____

I pledge to do my part to stop cyberbullying. I pledge to always think before I post a message or picture that can hurt myself or others. I also pledge to help a friend by notifying an adult or the school if someone is being cyberbullied.

Rewrite the pledge:

_____

_____

_____

Signature: _____ Date: _____

Cyberbullying Practice Scenarios

Scenario 1: You are at a party where other students are pressuring you to post a picture on social media that would embarrass another student. You feel pressured to fit in with the students.

What would you do if you were in this situation to prevent cyberbullying?

_____

_____

_____

_____

Scenario 2: Students at school are creating fake online accounts so they can post mean comments on other student online accounts without anyone knowing it is them. They ask you to participate in this with them.

What would you do if you were in this situation to prevent cyberbullying?

_____

_____

_____

_____

Scenario 3: A student is dating someone you like. You feel angry at this person and want to make up a rumor and share it through as many online outlets as possible. Your friends are encouraging you to do so.

What would you do if you were in this situation to prevent cyberbullying?

_____

_____

_____

_____

Book Study/Report Template

Steps

1. Research books written about this topic

2. Check out a book

3. Read the book

4. Complete the following, aligned with the book you read:

   ❑ Summary of the book

   ❑ Lessons learned from the book

   ❑ Identify ways this book can help other students in similar situations

   ❑ Suggestions for preventing this type of problem behavior in the future based on examples from the book

   ❑ Commitment from the student to never engage in this type of behavior again

   ❑ Create a flyer identifying the value of this book

Behavior Incident

DRUG/ALCOHOL OFFENSE

Suggestions for Alternatives

Reflective: Meet with a school or community police officer and gather information on the consequences of engaging in this type of behavior in the community. Write a two-page paper sharing what you learned from the police officer.

Instructional: Student will help plan and organize with the designated administrator or school staff on a drug-free campaign for the student body.

Restorative: Write apology letters to all stakeholders.

Reflective: Interview the school nurse about the effects of drug/alcohol on a child and write a one-page paper on what you learned from the interview.

Instructional: Research the dangers of underage drinking and the damage to the development of a child. Student will create a slide presentation and present it to the administrator and/or assigned classrooms/students.

Reflective: Student presents the research to a class (after proofed, as appropriate, by administrator) with the student's parents present.

Instructional: Six to eight sessions of behavior lessons practicing how to stand up to peer pressure and making the right decisions. Students will practice through scenarios where they are expected to apply the law to demonstrate what they've learned.

Restorative: Student assigned 20 hours of community service. Loss of privileges until the completion of all community service hours.

Restorative: Develop a student contract.

Instructional: Research a drug and alcohol policy in a selected workplace environment. Summarize the policy in a one-page paper and be prepared to present key findings.

Alcohol Assignment

Assignment: Research the answers to the questions provided.

1. What are the effects of alcohol on teenagers and adults?

   _____

   _____

   _____

2. What can happen if you mix alcohol with other drugs?

   _____

   _____

   _____

3. What are some of the short-term and long-term effects of alcohol?

   _____

   _____

   _____

4. What are ways alcohol can hurt you from reaching your goals?

   _____

   _____

   _____

5. What is the impact of alcohol abuse on family and friends?

   _____

   _____

   _____

6. What are the laws connected to alcohol?

   _____

   _____

   _____

7. What are some ways teachers and administrators can help prevent students from making poor decisions with alcohol?

   _____

   _____

   _____

8. What have you learned from this experience?

   _____

   _____

   _____

Law and Case Study Practice Worksheet

Assignment: Research three laws related to alcohol and drug offenses and summarize the laws.

Law:

_____

_____

Summary:

_____

_____

Law:

_____

_____

Summary:

_____

_____

Law:

_____

_____

Summary:

_____

_____

Read the case study and answer the questions.

Case Study: Jim and Joe have been best friends since the first grade. They strive for popularity at school and often test the boundaries of school rules. Jim called Joe on Sunday night to let him know he snuck some alcohol from a party his parents had the night before. The boys decide Jim is going to bring the beer he stole from the party to school the next day so they both can try it. At school, Jim brags that he brought alcohol and was showing it to other students. They went out at break to drink the beer, but before they took one sip, an adult on supervision heard about what they were doing and notified the administrator.

(Continued)

(Continued)

Case Study Questions

1. Have any laws been broken?

_____

_____

2. Why do you think the students behaved in the way that they did?

_____

_____

3. How do you think law enforcement would respond to this type of behavior?

_____

_____

4. Will the parents of these students be involved?

_____

_____

5. What do you think the students could have done instead?

_____

_____

6. What do you think is an appropriate consequence for these students?

_____

_____

7. What would help teach these students a lesson?

_____

_____

Drug and Alcohol Policy Assignment

Identify a workplace to be researched (e.g., Target employee, engineer, doctor, teacher):

_____

Research a drug and alcohol policy in your selected workplace environment. Summarize the policy and answer the questions.

Summary of the policy:

_____

_____

_____

_____

_____

_____

_____

1. What would happen if alcohol or drug abuse is observed during work hours on company premises?

   _____

   _____

2. What are some apparent physical states of impairment in employees using drugs or alcohol during work hours?

   _____

   _____

3. What do you think is the mental state of a person using drugs or alcohol at work?

   _____

   _____

(Continued)

(Continued)

4. What are some changes in personal behavior that would otherwise be unexplainable?

_____

_____

5. Do you think the use of drugs and alcohol can deteriorate a person's work performance?

_____

_____

6. What kind of accidents can occur in a workplace due to the use of drugs and alcohol?

_____

_____

7. What is a consequence for an employee who tests positive for drugs or alcohol in the workplace?

_____

_____

Behavior Incident

 # FIGHT

Suggestions for Alternatives

Restorative: The administrator will conduct a conflict resolution using a restorative approach to get to the root cause of the fight. This conflict resolution will be ongoing and up to three or four times to ensure the conflict is resolved over the next few weeks.

Restorative: The students will create and progress monitor a contract together with the supervision of an administrator for at least six weeks.

Instructional: Students will go through at least six sessions of hands-off academy behavior teaching lessons where they will learn and practice strategies before applying them to scenarios demonstrating mastery of learning.

Reflective: Students will be required to take an exit behavior exam demonstrating what they have learned from this experience prior to resuming full privileges on campus.

Instructional: Students will prepare a lesson and teach it to younger students or peers about the importance of solving problems appropriately.

Restorative: Students will have to write an apology letter to any stakeholders affected as a result of this behavior incident.

Reflective: Students will stay on a structured schedule until the completion of all requirements.

Restorative Contract

Date of Meeting: _____

Disputants

_____   _____   _____

_____   _____   _____

Referral Source

Administrator   Teacher   Student   Self   Other: _____

Conflict Information

What is the conflict about? _____

_____

_____

_____

_____

1. Did we recognize an injustice/violation?   Yes   No   Other: _____

2. Did we restore equity?   Yes   No

   Apology for injustices/violations: Yes   No

   Nothing beyond this meeting is necessary: Yes   No   Other: _____

3. Future Intentions (Agreement/Contract)

We agree to prevent this problem from happening again by: _____

_____

_____

_____

_____

_____

_____

Student Signatures: _____   _____   _____

(Continued)

(Continued)

4. Follow-Up Meeting

We agree to meet again for a follow-up meeting.

Follow-Up Meeting Date: _____

Student Signatures: _____ _____ _____

Follow-Up Results: _____

_____

_____

_____

_____

_____

_____

Behavior Exam

1. What happened that put you in this position?

   _____

   _____

   _____

   _____

2. What would you have done differently if you could go back and change what happened?

   _____

   _____

   _____

   _____

3. What did you learn from this experience? Provide three examples.

   _____

   _____

   _____

   _____

4. How can you assure the administration that you will not be a part of an incident such as this ever again? Provide three reasons.

   _____

   _____

   _____

   _____

5. How will you ensure that the student who was the victim of your behavior will not have to worry about you bothering him or her anymore? Provide three examples.

   _____

   _____

   _____

   _____

Hands-Off Academy: Weekly Self-Monitoring Form

Student Name: _____

Behaviors: How well did I . . .	Previous Week
Show respect to adults and students	Circle one: Good Fair Poor
Keep my hands to myself	Circle one: Good Fair Poor

What worked for you? _____

_____

What didn't work for you? _____

_____

Contract for This Week

I, _____, will work on _____ this week
in order to meet my behavior goal.

Administrator Signature: _____

Student Signature: _____

Behavior Incident

FIRE RELATED

Suggestions for Alternatives

Instructional: Student will contact the local fire department to research fire safety courses available to students. If available, have the student participate in the course and present what he learned to classmates or younger students.

Restorative: Student will write apology letters to all stakeholders.

Instructional: Student will interview and shadow the custodian for a week and will write a two-page paper describing the role of the custodian and how this type of behavior impacts his work.

Restorative: Student will complete restitution with the custodian decided by the administrator.

Reflective: Student will prepare and present a fire safety slide presentation.

Reflective: Student will interview a local family or someone you know who has lost their belongings or been impacted as the result of a fire and write a two-page reflection on what this experience has taught you.

Reflective: Student will research and write an essay on the consequences associated with fire-connected acts within the community.

Restorative: Student will research volunteer opportunities to help families who have lost valuables and so on in fire-related incidents.

Shadow Log

Assignment: Student will shadow designated adult for one week. He will log what he learned from the experience and will write a two-page reflection paper summarizing what he learned.

Date	Who Did You Shadow?	What Did You Learn?	Designated Adult Signature

Custodian Interview Questions

Assignment: Interview a custodian and summarize responses in a two-page reflection sheet.

1. What does your job entail on campus?

   _____

   _____

   _____

   _____

2. What are your experiences with fire-related incidents on campus?

   _____

   _____

   _____

   _____

3. How does a student engaging in a fire-related incident affect your work day?

   _____

   _____

   _____

   _____

4. What is in place to keep the school safe from fire-related incidents?

   _____

   _____

   _____

   _____

5. What do you think students can do to help prevent these types of incidents at school?

   _____

   _____

   _____

   _____

Fire-Related Slide Presentation Assignment Template

Date: _____

Student to complete and present a slide presentation that includes the following components:

- ❏ Topic: Fire-related incidents
- ❏ Overall question(s) to answer through research or educational course related to fire safety:

    What did you learn about fire safety that would be helpful to others?

    What are some tips to prevent fire-related incidents at school?

    What are some awareness activities that can help schools prevent fire-related incidents?

- ❏ Cite five research resources:

    _____

    _____

    _____

    _____

    _____

    _____

    _____

    _____

    _____

- ❏ Negative outcomes of engaging in this behavior
- ❏ Positive outcomes of not engaging in this behavior
- ❏ Methods to prevent this behavior in the future
- ❏ Final answer to the original overall question

Administrator Signature: _____

Student Signature: _____

Behavior Incident

INAPPROPRIATE LANGUAGE

Suggestions for Alternatives

Instructional: Student will be provided practice opportunities on how to rephrase inappropriate language to appropriate language.

Instructional: Student will teach younger grades appropriate language rules in school.

Reflective: Student will interview others around campus on how inappropriate language makes them feel.

Reflective: Student will complete an essay on how inappropriate language can affect their future in a workplace or within the community.

Reflective: Student will identify 10 positive appropriate words for each negative/inappropriate word used.

Instructional: Student will research the meaning of the language used (when appropriate) and create a presentation sharing history of the words.

Instructional: Student will complete six sessions of behavior lessons on self-control.

Restorative: Student will write apology letters to students and others offended by the language.

Restorative: Student will be placed on a language contract.

Reflective: Student will complete a respect reflection sheet.

Links for Behavior Lessons

http://www.pbisworld.com

http://www.pbisworld.com/tier-2/alternatives-to-suspension

http://www.pbischampionmodelsystem.com

https://www.goleaps.com

http://www.abesystems.com

http://www.mindsetworks.com/go?u=10

http://www.behavioradvisor.com/Contracts.html

http://specialed.about.com/library/templates/contract2.pdf

http://www.teachervision.fen.com/tv/printables/MENC_contract.pdf

http://www.usu.edu/teachall/text/behavior/LRBIpdfs/Behavioral.pdf

Respect Reflection Sheet

Name: _____

Write a plan on how you can be more respectful:

_____

_____

_____

_____

_____

_____

_____

What happens when you are not respectful?

_____

_____

_____

_____

_____

_____

_____

_____

What makes you a respectful person?

_____

_____

_____

_____

_____

_____

_____

(Continued)

(Continued)

Write three school rules that help everyone to be respectful:

_____

_____

_____

_____

_____

_____

What consequences should be in place for students who are not respectful?

_____

_____

_____

_____

_____

_____

Give me some examples of things that **are** and **are not** respectful:

_____   _____

_____   _____

_____   _____

_____   _____

On another page, make a poster about being respectful.

Inappropriate Language Worksheet

Write down the inappropriate language used:

_____

_____

_____

Write three other ways you can communicate what you meant appropriately:

1. _____

2. _____

3. _____

Write the inappropriate word(s) that was said toward another student:

_____

_____

_____

Write five positive words in place of this word(s) used toward the other student:

1. _____

2. _____

3. _____

4. _____

5. _____

Behavior Incident

 # PROPERTY DAMAGE

Suggestions for Alternatives

Reflective: Interview the student to figure out the reason he or she caused the damage.

Restorative: Student will apologize to the custodian and other stakeholders in person or through an apology letter.

Restorative: Student will be assigned restitution for 15 days or administrator-decided length of time based on the damage. The custodian or another stakeholder will supervise the student and sign off on restitution work and attitude of the student during restitution. The student will write a thank-you letter after the completion of restitution to show their appreciation and understanding of this life lesson.

Instructional: Student will research the cost of damage and work with stakeholders to develop a workplan for correcting the damage. The action plan will be presented to the administrator and stakeholders.

Instructional: Student will complete six to eight sessions of behavior academy or teaching opportunity, providing student scenarios to help him or her see the affects of his or her behavior on others and to learn self-control skills.

Instructional: Administrator will print examples of local stores that have been vandalized for the student to research and learn the impact vandalism has on others. Student will write an essay demonstrating empathy with evidence from the local examples.

Instructional: Student will research adult consequences for property damage and write a one-page reflection on how this type of behavior can impact a person's life in a negative way.

Restorative: Develop a contract with monitoring by the administration for at least six to eight weeks.

Property Damage Audit

Assignment: Research the cost of damage and work with assigned stakeholder to develop an action plan for improvement. Write a two-page paper describing your experience with this damage audit and the completion of the damage cleanup.

Property Damage Clean-Up Action Plan

Action Type			
Finding			
Root Cause			
Proposed Action			
Due Date		**Task Assigned To**	
Completion Date		**Task Approved By**	
Final Action			
Action Effectiveness			
Evaluation Date		**Task Approved By**	

Property Damage Practice Scenarios

Scenario 1: Your friends are bored over the weekend. One friend suggests to go vandalize your school. All of your friends seem to be on board with this plan.

What would you do if you were in this situation to prevent property damage?

_____

_____

_____

_____

Scenario 2: You know that no one is monitoring the bathrooms after lunch. You are mad at a student and want to write degrading messages about him or her in the bathroom.

What would you do if you were in this situation to prevent property damage?

_____

_____

_____

_____

Scenario 3: The teacher you do not like leaves the classroom unsupervised. You know you have access to do as you wish to her classroom items. Your friends are pressuring you to do so.

What would you do if you were in this situation to prevent property damage?

_____

_____

_____

_____

Restitution Monitoring Sheet

Amount of restitution assigned: _____

Restitution description: _____

What was the behavior that resulted in restitution? _____

Supervisor name: _____

Date/Restitution Amount Served	Did I complete my assigned restitution with quality effort? (Yes or No) Supervisor Signature	Did I complete my assigned restitution with a good attitude? (Yes or No) Supervisor Signature

After the completion of your restitution, write a one-page reflection to your restitution supervisor thanking him or her for the opportunity and sharing with them what you have learned from this experience.

Behavior Incident

💼 REPEATED CLASSROOM DISRUPTIONS

Suggestions for Alternatives

Restorative: Student will be placed on a classroom contract developed with the teacher and monitored on a daily basis.

Restorative: Student will be placed on a restorative agreement with the teacher and coordinated with the support of an administrator to ensure the relationship is restored.

Restorative: Student will write an apology letter to the teacher.

Reflective: Student will be placed on Check-in/Check-out targeted intervention designed for additional structure and increased positive adult interaction for six to eight weeks (Todd, Campbell, Meyer, & Horner, 2008).

Instructional: Student will receive six to eight sessions of behavior academy lessons to teach the student how to follow classroom rules and contract.

Restorative: Student will complete restitution in the classroom or around school (based on teacher and administration).

Reflective: Student will complete a behavior exam for the student to apply learned skills.

Reflective: Student will have an alternative zone to complete work and practice replacement behaviors learned in behavior academies.

Reflective: Student will complete a "Write 'Your New Story' Prompt" form and present what he or she wrote with the teacher and administrator.

Check-In/Check-Out Monitoring Form

Date: _____	Be Respectful	Be Safe	Work Peacefully	Strive for Excellence	Follow Directions	Teacher Initials
8:45 – A.M. Break	0 1 2	0 1 2	0 1 2	0 1 2	0 1 2	
A.M. Break – 12:00	0 1 2	0 1 2	0 1 2	0 1 2	0 1 2	
12:00 – Lunch	0 1 2	0 1 2	0 1 2	0 1 2	0 1 2	
Lunch – End of Day	0 1 2	0 1 2	0 1 2	0 1 2	0 1 2	

Total Points: _____ Possible Points: 40 Today: ____% **Goal: 70% or 28/40 points**

Date: _____	Be Respectful	Be Safe	Work Peacefully	Strive for Excellence	Follow Directions	Teacher Initials
8:45 – A.M. Break	0 1 2	0 1 2	0 1 2	0 1 2	0 1 2	
A.M. Break – 12:00	0 1 2	0 1 2	0 1 2	0 1 2	0 1 2	
12:00 – Lunch	0 1 2	0 1 2	0 1 2	0 1 2	0 1 2	
Lunch – End of Day	0 1 2	0 1 2	0 1 2	0 1 2	0 1 2	

Total Points: _____ Possible Points: 40 Today: ____% **Goal: 70% or 28/40 points**

Date: _____	Be Respectful	Be Safe	Work Peacefully	Strive for Excellence	Follow Directions	Teacher Initials
8:45 – A.M. Break	0 1 2	0 1 2	0 1 2	0 1 2	0 1 2	
A.M. Break – 12:00	0 1 2	0 1 2	0 1 2	0 1 2	0 1 2	
12:00 – End of Day	0 1 2	0 1 2	0 1 2	0 1 2	0 1 2	

Total Points: _____ Possible Points: 30 Today: ____% **Goal: 70% or 21/30 points**

Date: _____	Be Respectful	Be Safe	Work Peacefully	Strive for Excellence	Follow Directions	Teacher Initials
8:45 – A.M. Break	0 1 2	0 1 2	0 1 2	0 1 2	0 1 2	
A.M. Break – 12:00	0 1 2	0 1 2	0 1 2	0 1 2	0 1 2	
12:00 – Lunch	0 1 2	0 1 2	0 1 2	0 1 2	0 1 2	
Lunch – End of Day	0 1 2	0 1 2	0 1 2	0 1 2	0 1 2	

Total Points: _____ Possible Points: 40 Today: ____% **Goal: 70% or 28/40 points**

Date: _____	Be Respectful	Be Safe	Work Peacefully	Strive for Excellence	Follow Directions	Teacher Initials
8:45 – A.M. Break	0 1 2	0 1 2	0 1 2	0 1 2	0 1 2	
A.M. Break – 12:00	0 1 2	0 1 2	0 1 2	0 1 2	0 1 2	
12:00 – Lunch	0 1 2	0 1 2	0 1 2	0 1 2	0 1 2	
Lunch – End of Day	0 1 2	0 1 2	0 1 2	0 1 2	0 1 2	

Total Points: _____ Possible Points: 40 Today: ____% **Goal: 70% or 28/40 points**

0 = Poor   1 = Fair   2 = Great Job!

Write "Your New Story" Prompt

Name: _____ Date: _____

Who am I . . .

_____

_____

_____

_____

_____

_____

What are some poor choices I have made in the past at school (*my old story*)?

_____

_____

_____

_____

_____

_____

What do I want to see for myself (*my new story*) when it comes to behavior and academics in school?

_____

_____

_____

_____

_____

_____

_____

(Continued)

(Continued)

How do I plan on making this *new story* come true?

_____

_____

_____

_____

_____

_____

_____

What help do I need to make this *new story* come true?

_____

_____

_____

_____

_____

_____

_____

Student signature of commitment to *My New Story:* _____

Alternative Zone

Beginning Date: _____   Ending Date: _____

This alternative zone is designed to give the student an opportunity to practice their learned replacement behaviors from behavior academy and to provide an alternative zone that can be utilized through teacher and/or student request to go to a safe space to complete organized assignments with adult supervision instead of disruptive behavior escalating in class. The goal is for the student to decrease the amount of times he or she goes into this alternative zone location.

> **Important note to consider throughout the day: Alternative Zone (designated location with structured assignments and designated adult support)**
>
> If the student is disrupting teaching or about to engage in attention-seeking behavior with the teacher (power struggle), the teacher will send the student with a red folder to the designated location. The teacher is to make a phone call to the office with a selected code for someone to come help with the situation if the teacher perceives this will trigger the student's behavior.
>
> If the student is at a point where he or she needs to be removed, the following are examples of structured assignments to be completed: Read Accelerated Reader book (take notes, pass a quiz), online math intervention (40 minutes), online reading intervention (40 minutes), math facts practice, essay on appropriate behavior, or any incomplete work the teacher wants completed.

Progress Monitoring

(Administrator to fill out and track the number of times in each day the student went to the Alternative Zone)

Dates:	How many times did student go to the Alternative Zone?	Was the plan followed with fidelity today?			
Week:		Student	Teacher	Parent	Admin
Monday					
Tuesday					
Wednesday					
Thursday					
Friday					

Behavior Incident

SEXUAL HARASSMENT

Suggestions for Alternatives

Restorative: A restorative agreement will be completed between the students.

Restorative: Student will write apology letters to all stakeholders.

Reflective: Student will interview important women in his or her life and ask how they would feel if someone sexually harassed them. Student will present what he or she learned to the administrator.

Instructional: Student will research the district handbook description on sexual harassment and identify a sexual harassment policy in a work environment. Student will write an essay describing what was learned and the consequences connected to engaging in these types of behaviors within the community.

Instructional: Student is assigned four sessions with a designated school employee to role-play appropriate ways of seeking peer attention from other students. In these sessions, student will be provided scenarios and taught strategies to handle them appropriately.

Restorative: Student will meet with the victim in a safe, supervised place with the administrator present to share what was learned from this experience and how it will not continue.

Reflective: Student will create an individual behavior contract identifying his or her commitment to changing their behavior.

Instructional: Student will visit the U.S. Department of Justice website to research prevention on violence against women and present findings and laws to the administrator.

Reflective: Student will be given a structured schedule with check-ins set up for six to eight weeks with the administrator.

Student Contract Template

Date of Contract: _____

Contract Monitoring Dates:

_____   _____   _____   _____   _____   _____

I, _____, am writing this contract to assure that I will not engage in the behavior that resulted in hurting myself or others again. The behavior I was engaged in included _____, and I hurt _____ _____ by engaging in this behavior. I am going to take the following actions to ensure I will never engage in this behavior again:

Identified Actions

1. _____

2. _____

3. _____

4. _____

5. _____

I will ensure I am following my identified actions by:

_____

_____

I will monitor how I am doing with my contract by:

_____

_____

I will need help with the following to make sure I follow my identified actions:

_____

_____

I believe the following needs to take place if I do not follow my contract:

_____

_____

Student Signature: _____

Administrator Signature: _____

Project Assignment Template

Problem behavior: (e.g., sexual harassment) _____

Possible function of behavior: (e.g., attention seeking, lack of social skills) _____

_____

Date to complete by: _____

Project Assignment

1. Research two sexual harassment descriptions or policies and respond to the following writing prompts: What were commonalities between the policies? What are some ways to prevent sexual harassment? What have you learned from this assignment?

   _____

   _____

   _____

   _____

2. Research sexual harassment laws. List three laws created to prevent sexual harassment in the workplace. Provide examples of how to follow the laws.

   _____

   _____

   _____

   _____

3. Develop a project to create sexual harassment prevention awareness. Project needs to include the following: definition of sexual harassment, ways to prevent sexual harassment, and lessons learned.

   _____

   _____

   _____

   _____

Administrator Signature: _____

Stakeholder Signature(s): _____

Student(s) Signature: _____

Sample Structured Schedule

Beginning Date: _____   Ending Date:_____

Where am I supposed to report and what am I doing during the following times of the school day. . . .

Before-School Check-In: _____

Class: _____

Morning Recess: _____

Class: _____

Lunch and Lunch Recess: _____

After-School Check-Out: _____

Date	Did I check in this morning? (Yes or No) Administrator or Designee Signature	Did I follow my schedule today with no problems? (Yes or No) Administrator or Designee Signature
10 pass days earns privileges back to the student		

Behavior Incident

SUBSTITUTE TEACHER

Suggestions for Alternatives

Restorative: Student will write an apology letter to the substitute teacher.

Restorative: Student will complete classroom restitution with the administrator, teacher, and student.

Reflective: Student will write the rules and expectations of the class when a substitute is present.

Instructional: Student will create an assignment for his or her classmates to participate in. The assignment will be led by the student on the topic of appropriate ways to behave with a substitute teacher in class.

Instructional: Student will research substitute teacher job description and present the requirements to the administrator.

Reflective: Student will interview a substitute teacher and write a one-page reflection of the challenges and opportunities that come with substitute teaching.

Reflective: Student will interview five students on appropriate ways to behave when a substitute teacher is in class and prepare a handout that highlights 10 ways to behave with a substitute teacher.

Restorative: The student will facilitate a classroom substitute teacher contract discussion that will be reviewed the morning any substitute teacher enters the classroom.

Restorative: Student will be assigned five mornings of welcoming a substitute teacher on campus (in any grade), where the student is required to share school behavior expectations and rules and walk them to their classroom after the check-in.

Classroom Substitute Teacher Contract

Assignment: The student is to guide classmates through the following questions, then develop a classroom contract with the collected information signed by all students and posted in the classroom. The student is to review the substitute teacher contract with their class prior to having a substitute teacher in class to reinforce the contract.

Facilitating Questions

- How should we behave when a substitute teacher is in our class?

- What are some behaviors that should not take place when we have a substitute teacher?

- What does it look like to show respect to the substitute teacher?

- What can we commit to doing when we have a substitute teacher?

- Why is it important to treat a substitute teacher in this way?

- How can we make sure we are respecting this contract?

Substitute Teacher Interview Questions

Assignment: Interview a substitute teacher and write a two-page reflection addressing the following questions using evidence from the interview. Provide a copy of the reflection to the teacher, interviewed substitute teacher, and administrator.

1. What are some challenges of being a substitute teacher?

2. What are some opportunities of being a substitute teacher?

3. How should students behave when they have a substitute teacher?

Substitute Teacher Interview Questions

- Why did you get into substitute teaching?

- How do you expect students to behave when you are substitute teaching?

- Have you experienced disrespectful students while you were substitute teaching?

- How do you feel when students are not following classroom rules when you are substitute teaching?

- Have you had positive experiences substitute teaching?

- What would be your ideal classroom to substitute for?

Develop three additional questions to ask the substitute teacher:

1. _____

2. _____

3. _____

Substitute Welcoming Monitoring Chart

Assignment: Five mornings of welcoming a substitute teacher on campus, where the student is required to share school behavior expectations and rules before walking them to their classroom after the check-in. Provide a one-page reflection of this experience to the administrator after all five days of substitute welcoming committee time is completed.

Student Name: _____

Date	Substitute teacher name and classroom subbing in	Substitute teacher signature after being provided with an overview of the behavior expectations and rules and walked to the classroom	Administrator or designee signature

Behavior Incident

TECHNOLOGY OFFENSE

Suggestions for Alternatives

Reflective: Student will review the school handbook or provided technology rules/policies and write a one-page reflection on the appropriate ways to use technology.

Restorative: Student will be assigned to assist the site technician or designated teacher on campus with technology support for four weeks during recess/break/lunch. Student will have loss of privileges until restitution is completed.

Reflective: Student will write a two-page paper on how to use technology appropriately, specifically referencing incidents where students abused technology and the impact that abuse had on the school's ability to make technology accessible to all students.

Instructional: Student will develop a slide presentation to educate other students on the appropriate use of technology.

Restorative: Student will develop a technology contract that is monitored by the student and administration to ensure this will not happen again.

Reflective: Student will undergo a daily technology check-in and check-out for four to six weeks to ensure there has not been any inappropriate searches or use.

Instructional: Student will work with administrator or assigned teacher on a technology lesson for teachers, helping them see ways students can abuse technology so they are prepared to be proactive. Student will present at a staff meeting or other approved time for teacher professional development. This presentation may also be created in a webinar or video format.

Slide Presentation Assignment Template

Date: _____

Student to complete and present a slide presentation that includes the following components:

❑ Topic (e.g., student aggression, cyberbullying, theft):

_____

❑ Overall question to answer through research (e.g., How do we prevent technology offenses in school? How can we help teachers and administrators become aware of technology offenses? How can we help teachers and administrators become preventive when using technology in their classrooms?)

❑ Six examples of the resources used to prepare this presentation, along with evidence:

_____

_____

_____

_____

_____

_____

❑ Negative outcomes of engaging in this behavior

❑ Positive outcomes of not engaging in this behavior

❑ Methods to prevent this behavior in the future

❑ Final answer to the overall question

Administrator Signature: _____

Student Signature: _____

Reflection Paper Template

Assignment: Review the school handbook or provided technology rules/policies and write a one-page reflection on how to use technology appropriately. The completed reflection will be approved by the administrator and must include the following components:

❒ Describe the behavior that resulted in the misuse of technology.

❒ Describe what you could have done instead to avoid being in this position.

❒ Summarize the information provided to you for review.

❒ Provide three example scenarios of inappropriate technology offenses in schools and provide an explanation of how to prevent these types of technology offenses from occurring.

❒ Provide suggestions and tips for teachers and administrators on how to prevent technology offenses in schools.

❒ Describe how you plan to avoid inappropriate uses of technology in the future.

❒ Describe what you learned from this experience.

Technology Contract Template

I, _____, was engaged in using technology inappropriately, which resulted in a consequence at school. I understand I made a poor decision by engaging in this behavior and, therefore, I commit to the following to ensure that I will never participate in this type of behavior again:

1. _____

2. _____

3. _____

4. _____

5. _____

I am committing to monitor my technology contract on a weekly basis with the designated school faculty member assigned to ensure my contract is being honored.

Week of . . .	Did I follow my contract? (Yes or No) School Designee Signature
Week 1	
Week 2	
Week 3	
Week 4	
Week 5	
Week 6	

Student Signature: _____

Administrator Signature: _____

School Designee Signature: _____

Behavior Incident

THEFT

Suggestions for Alternatives

Reflective: Interview the student to identify the root of why the student stole the item.

Restorative: Provide an opportunity for the student who stole to apologize to the person(s) he or she stole from.

Reflective: Student will undergo morning and after-school check-ins with administration to ensure there are no stolen items leaving the campus. Process is approved by parents/guardians to continue for six to eight weeks.

Instructional: Student will research the average amount of community service assigned to an adult who steals in the community. Student will write a one-page reflection on findings and a community service proposal to be followed during restitution on campus.

Restorative: Student will complete community service/restitution on campus. The time of service will be aligned to the cost of stolen item. Student will have loss of privileges until community service and assignments are completed.

Instructional: Student will complete six sessions of behavior academies or opportunities focused on appropriate ways to earn what you want in school, home, and community.

Reflective: A classroom behavior contract will be developed with the teacher. It will be monitored on a daily and weekly basis.

Reflective: Student will be assigned a mentor on campus to provide support for the student with weekly check-ins with the mentor to ensure student is on track. Student is encouraged to provide feedback to a mentor who he or she respects.

Reflective: School will work with parents to provide family support if this is a common behavior happening at school, home, and community. Student will be assigned 10 days of journal entries that will include parent/guardian input.

Instructional: The student will write an essay on the importance of trust, with evidence demonstrating learning from this experience. The assignment will be signed off by the teacher and administration.

Community Service Form

Student Name: _____ Grade:_____

Date Service Begins: _____

Hours or Days Assigned:

_____ Total hours of service assigned

_____ Total days of service assigned

Community Service Job Description:

_____

_____

Community Service Supervisor: _____

Date	Location of Service	Time or Days (e.g., 3 hours or a full day)	Staff Initials	Additional Comments

At the completion of service, student will submit a reflection on what he or she learned from this experience, and an administrator, supervisor, parent, and student need to sign this document.

Administrator Signature: _____

Community Service Supervisor Signature: _____

Parent Signature: _____

Student Signature: _____

Check-In Monitoring Form

Date	Morning: Did I have anything in my possession that did not belong to me? (Yes or No) Staff Initials	Afternoon: Did I have anything in my possession that did not belong to me? (Yes or No) Staff Initials

Student Interview Questions: Theft

- Explain what took place from your side of the story.

- What made you take the item?

- Did you feel bad about taking the item?

- Did you ever consider returning the item?

- Do you think people have lost trust in you due to your behavior?

- What are you going to do to earn trust back?

- Has anyone stolen anything from you before? If yes, how did it make you feel?

- What do you think is an appropriate consequence for your behavior?

- Have you stolen items before?

- What type of help do you think you need to stop you from taking items from others?

- What do you think would happen if you got caught stealing something in the community?

- What are your plans to restore the relationship with the person(s) you stole from?

- Do you have any questions for me?

Behavior Incident

TRUANCY

Suggestions for Alternatives

Restorative: Student will be assigned a job at school with a designated supervisor for six weeks.

Restorative: Student will receive community service hours for the amount of school missed.

Instructional: Student will receive six to eight sessions of behavior lessons targeting organization, time management, and motivation.

Reflective: Student is required to have daily check-ins with designated school personnel.

Instructional: Student will research how truancy (absenteeism) can impact a career as an adult.

Instructional: Student will research and develop tips to prevent truancy that will be used as a guide for other students.

Reflective: Truancy contract will be developed with student input and monitored daily.

Truancy Progress Monitoring Sheet

Week of	Monday	Tuesday	Wednesday	Thursday	Friday	Point total	Did I meet my goal this week? (Yes or No)
Week 1	On time **Yes (1) or No (0)** Work completion progress **Yes (1) or No (0)**	On time **Yes (1) or No (0)** Work completion progress **Yes (1) or No (0)**	On time **Yes (1) or No (0)** Work completion progress **Yes (1) or No (0)**	On time **Yes (1) or No (0)** Work completion progress **Yes (1) or No (0)**	On time **Yes (1) or No (0)** Work completion progress **Yes (1) or No (0)**		
Week 2	On time **Yes (1) or No (0)** Work completion progress **Yes (1) or No (0)**	On time **Yes (1) or No (0)** Work completion progress **Yes (1) or No (0)**	On time **Yes (1) or No (0)** Work completion progress **Yes (1) or No (0)**	On time **Yes (1) or No (0)** Work completion progress **Yes (1) or No (0)**	On time **Yes (1) or No (0)** Work completion progress **Yes (1) or No (0)**		
Week 3	On time **Yes (1) or No (0)** Work completion progress **Yes (1) or No (0)**	On time **Yes (1) or No (0)** Work completion progress **Yes (1) or No (0)**	On time **Yes (1) or No (0)** Work completion progress **Yes (1) or No (0)**	On time **Yes (1) or No (0)** Work completion progress **Yes (1) or No (0)**	On time **Yes (1) or No (0)** Work completion progress **Yes (1) or No (0)**		
Week 4	On time **Yes (1) or No (0)** Work completion progress **Yes (1) or No (0)**	On time **Yes (1) or No (0)** Work completion progress **Yes (1) or No (0)**	On time **Yes (1) or No (0)** Work completion progress **Yes (1) or No (0)**	On time **Yes (1) or No (0)** Work completion progress **Yes (1) or No (0)**	On time **Yes (1) or No (0)** Work completion progress **Yes (1) or No (0)**		
Week 5	On time **Yes (1) or No (0)** Work completion progress **Yes (1) or No (0)**	On time **Yes (1) or No (0)** Work completion progress **Yes (1) or No (0)**	On time **Yes (1) or No (0)** Work completion progress **Yes (1) or No (0)**	On time **Yes (1) or No (0)** Work completion progress **Yes (1) or No (0)**	On time **Yes (1) or No (0)** Work completion progress **Yes (1) or No (0)**		
Week 6	On time **Yes (1) or No (0)** Work completion progress **Yes (1) or No (0)**	On time **Yes (1) or No (0)** Work completion progress **Yes (1) or No (0)**	On time **Yes (1) or No (0)** Work completion progress **Yes (1) or No (0)**	On time **Yes (1) or No (0)** Work completion progress **Yes (1) or No (0)**	On time **Yes (1) or No (0)** Work completion progress **Yes (1) or No (0)**		

Note: 8/10 points in a week = end of the day and end of week small student-selected incentive from administrator

Behavior Worksheet: Time Management Skills

What is the definition of time management?

- How do you think time management is related to your truancy difficulties?

- What are factors preventing you from being on time and at school?

- What are factors contributing to you not getting to school on time?

- What are some ways to improve your attendance and tardiness?

- What can a school staff member help you with in order to improve your truancy?

Research the following and write a summary for each:

1. Research time management skills and write a summary of how you plan on implementing these learned skills.

2. Research what would happen to you if you were continuously late to your job in your future career, and write a summary about what you plan to do to prevent this from happening to you.

3. Research ways to keep up with your school workload, and write a summary of how you plan on utilizing school resources to catch up.

Student Contract Template

Truancy Contract Sample

Date of Contract: _____

Monitoring Dates: _____ _____ _____ _____ _____

I, _____, am writing this contract to assure that I will improve my truancy. The truancy behavior I was engaged in that resulted in this contract includes _____. This behavior has hurt my educational progress by _____. I am going to take the following actions to ensure I will improve my truancy:

Identified Actions

1. _____

2. _____

3. _____

4. _____

5. _____

I will ensure I am following my identified actions by:

_____

_____

I will monitor how I am doing with my contract by:

_____

_____

I will need help with the following to make sure I adhere to my identified actions:

_____

_____

I believe the following needs to take place if I do not honor this contract:

_____

_____

Student Signature: _____

Administrator Signature: _____

PART IV

Bringing It All Together

So What Now?

You have been given a lot of information to process in this book. Do not feel overwhelmed at this point. Challenge yourself to use the alternative/innovative discipline frame as a guide to help assign meaningful discipline. For educators who are ready to take this step, you will see a difference in how you work with students after the first time you successfully assign discipline this way. As educators, we have a moral imperative to reach *all* students academically and behaviorally. Our school/district mission and vision statements *say* all students, every day, but do our actions support it? Sending a student home repeatedly for behavior certainly doesn't support these statements. We understand using discipline as a teaching opportunity to change behavior will feel unusual and uncomfortable at first, but isn't this the case for all educational practices needing a facelift? As educators, we must continue to evolve every day (not just in our words, but our actions) to keep up with the increasingly complex and challenging needs of our students. These opportunities aren't given to students by chance, but through an intentional focus and design.

As you begin this journey ask yourself the following reflective questions:

1. Do you believe in doing discipline in this way?

2. Is creating and maintaining a solid foundational behavior system at your school a priority?

3. Are you willing to allocate time and resources to this form of discipline?

4. Have you analyzed your school discipline data for disproportionality in students of color?

5. Are you ready for challenging courageous conversations?

6. Are you ready to change lives?

Use the following template to organize alternative discipline assignments. This will ensure each necessary component is addressed when assigning discipline. Use the menu of alternatives as a guide to select each appropriate response for your student.

Alternative Discipline Contract

Student Name: _____

Assigning Administrator(s): _____

Beginning Date: _____

Behavior Description:

_____

_____

_____

_____

Perceived Function of the Behavior:

_____

_____

_____

Alternative Discipline Delivery Phases (Note: Educator has discretion on how many phases to use for the delivery of the alternative discipline. Recommended to have at least three phases):

Phases of the Alternative Discipline	Responsible Person(s)	Date to Be Completed By	Phase Completed: Yes or No
Phase 1:			
Phase 2:			
Phase 3:			
Phase 4:			
Phase 5:			

What part of the consequence is restorative?

_____

_____

_____

_____

(Continued)

(Continued)

What part of the consequence is reflective?

_____

_____

_____

_____

What part of the consequence is instructional?

_____

_____

_____

_____

Additional comments or notes:

_____

_____

_____

_____

_____

_____

_____

_____

_____

Student Signature: _____

Administrator Signature: _____

Other Signature: _____

CHALLENGE TO EDUCATORS

We challenge educators to go above and beyond when addressing student behavior. A student's brain is not fully developed until early adulthood; they will make mistakes and need support from adults to help learn from those mistakes. We as educators must teach them how to act, how to make good decisions, and to succeed in the real world. We cannot expect this to happen while not supporting a student's social-emotional development. We cannot give *all* students the opportunity to learn and behave through punitive exclusionary contexts. Follow the guidelines provided in this book and invest with sincere commitment, and you will see what we refer to as the "Art of Discipline."

I commit to using alternative/innovative discipline in my school or district by:

_____

_____

_____

_____

_____

_____

After using this approach, I found that:

_____

_____

_____

_____

_____

_____

References

Balfanz, R., & Boccanfuso, C. (2007). *Falling off the path to graduation: Early indicators brief.* Baltimore, MD: Everyone Graduates Center.

Chard, D., Smith, S., & Sugai, G. (1992). Packaged discipline programs: A consumer's guide. In J. Marr & G. Tindal (Eds.) *1992 Oregon conference monograph* (pp. 19–27). Eugene, OR: University of Oregon.

Hannigan, J., & Hauser, L. (2014). *The PBIS tier one handbook: A practical approach to implementing the champion model.* Thousand Oaks, CA: Corwin.

Irvin, L. K., Tobin, T. J., Sprague, J. R., Sugai, G., & Vincent, C. G. (2004). Validity of office discipline referral measures as indices of school-wide behavioral status and effects of school-wide behavioral interventions. *Journal of Positive Behavior Interventions, 6*(3), 131–147.

Leone, P. E., Christle, C. A., Nelson, M., Skiba, R., Frey, A., & Jolivette, K. (2003). *School failure, race and disability: Promoting positive outcomes, decreasing vulnerability for involvement with the juvenile delinquency system.* College Park, MD: The National Center on Education, Disability, and Juvenile Justice.

Losen, D. J. (2011). *Discipline policies, successful schools and racial justice.* Boulder, CO: National Education Policy Center, School of Education, University of Colorado Boulder.

Mayer, G. R. (1995). Preventing antisocial behavior in the schools. *Journal of Applied Behavior Analysis, 28*(4), 467–478.

McCook, J. E. (2006). *The RTI guide: Developing and implementing a model in your schools.* Palm Beach Gardens, FL: LRP Publications.

Perry, B. L., & Morris, E. W. (2014). Suspending progress: Collateral consequences of exclusionary punishment in public schools. *American Sociological Review, 79*(6). doi:0003122414556308

Skiba, R., & Peterson, R. (1999). The dark side of zero tolerance: Can punishment lead to safe schools? *Phi Delta Kappan,* 372–382.

Skiba, R. J., & Rausch, M. K. (2006). Zero tolerance, suspension, and expulsion: Questions of equity and effectiveness. *Handbook of Classroom Management: Research, Practice, and Contemporary Issues,* 1063–1089.

Todd, A. W., Campbell, A. L., Meyer, G. G., & Horner, R. H. (2008). The effects of a targeted intervention to reduce problem behaviors: Elementary school implementation of check in—check out. *Journal of Positive Behavior Interventions, 10*(1), 46–55.

Wald, J., & Losen, D. (2003). *Deconstructing the school-to-prison pipeline: New directions for youth development.* San Francisco, CA: Jossey-Bass.

Index

A SAGE Publishing Company

Helping educators make the greatest impact

CORWIN HAS ONE MISSION: to enhance education through intentional professional learning.

We build long-term relationships with our authors, educators, clients, and associations who partner with us to develop and continuously improve the best evidence-based practices that establish and support lifelong learning.